MY MUMMY'S GOT TATTOOS

Story by Andy White
Illustrations by Anita Lester
Design by Emma Byrne

Copyright © 2014 Andy White

First Australian print run.
Limited Edition of 1,000 copies.

ISBN: 978-1-925171-67-9

Published by Vivid Publishing
P.O. Box 948, Fremantle
Western Australia 6959
www.vividpublishing.com.au

Cataloguing-in-publication data is held at the National Library of Australia.

ACKNOWLEDGEMENTS
Paul & Robyn White, Jo Simpson, Nick Reid @ SKUNX Tattoos London, Hal Cheshire @ Tattoos From Hal & Green Lotus Tattoos Melbourne, Tashi Dukanovic @ Green Lotus Tattoos Melbourne, Tania Jovanovic, Liam Wood, Oliver Smith, Kevin Mack @ Tatsup Premium Tattoo Supplies, Lee Stain @ INKTRICATE Melbourne, Grace & Gabe @ Café Romantica, Everybody @ Code Black Coffee, Jason Swiney @ VIVID Publishing. All those whose faith in this project has helped keep me going throughout this journey.
Cheers. Feel the love, Andy White

Story and illustrations © 2014 Andy White @ CELEBRITIES ANONYMOUS.

All rights reserved. No part of this publication may be reproduced, stored in a retrieval system or transmitted in any form or by any means, electronic, mechanical, photocopying, recording or otherwise, without the prior written permission of the copyright holder.

For Toby and Harvey

My Mummy looks different to some other Mummies.

That's because my Mummy's got tattoos.

Some of them are scary, some are crazy,
some are big and some of them are small.
Some are pictures and some are patterns.
Some of them are words or numbers.

Mummy has a mermaid on her arm that makes bath time fun. We sing songs and pretend that the mermaid is joining in with our singing. Sometimes the mermaid does a dance with the toys in the bathtub. Sometimes the mermaid has swimming races with the toys too.

When Mummy reads me stories, I pretend that Mummy's tattoos join in the story with the pictures in the book. Sometimes I see Little Red Riding Hood and Pin-Ups scaring away the Big Bad Wolf with their Kung Fu skills. Sometimes I see The Three Little Pigs flying up high in a hot air balloon.

I like looking at all the pictures on Mummy's arms. They are magical. While we are all asleep they come alive and go on adventures.

Mummy says that as soon as I fall asleep some of them come into my bedroom to make sure no monsters can ever come to eat me up. I'm glad my Mummy's got tattoos because I don't want to be eaten by monsters.

Uncle Matthew thinks Mummy's tattoos are silly and she should grow up. He does not have any tattoos and Mummy says, "He's just being silly."

Uncle Matthew always says, "No, that's not it at all. Your Mummy will always be my silly younger sister who should grow up."

But I love my Mummy just the way she is.

Uncle Josh also has lots of tattoos. I think he's really nice because he's our family doctor and helps make us better when we are sick. Every time we visit his office he gives me a lollypop. I love lollypops.

Uncle Josh isn't like Uncle Matthew because he thinks Mummy's tattoos are cool. Uncle Josh thinks my Mummy should never grow up. Sometimes they both act like children. I think it's funny when they do.

When I was born Mummy got my name tattooed in a love heart. She said she did that because she wants the whole world to know she is going to love me forever. She did the same when my baby brother was born too.

Sometimes Mummy lets me put on fake tattoos and we play a joke on Grandma. I say to her, "Look Grandma, I've got tattoos. Just like Mummy's."

Grandma always shakes her head and says, "You can't fool Grandma. And because you tried to, I'm going to tickle you now."

Then she holds me down and tickles me until I nearly wee my pants.

When we go shopping at the supermarket, sometimes people point and stare at Mummy's tattoos.

This makes Mummy smile and say, "It's okay, I don't mind what they say. I know I look funny to some people. But everyone looks funny to someone."

So, I always say to her, "I don't think you look funny Mummy."

"Thank you. That's because you're seriously SUPER DUPER COOL," she says back as she gives me a big hug. Then she lets me choose something sweet to eat as a treat after dinner.

Some people don't like my Mummy's tattoos but I don't care because she's my Mummy.

Every day I tell my Mummy, "I love you and I love your tattoos." Then I give her a big hug and kiss.

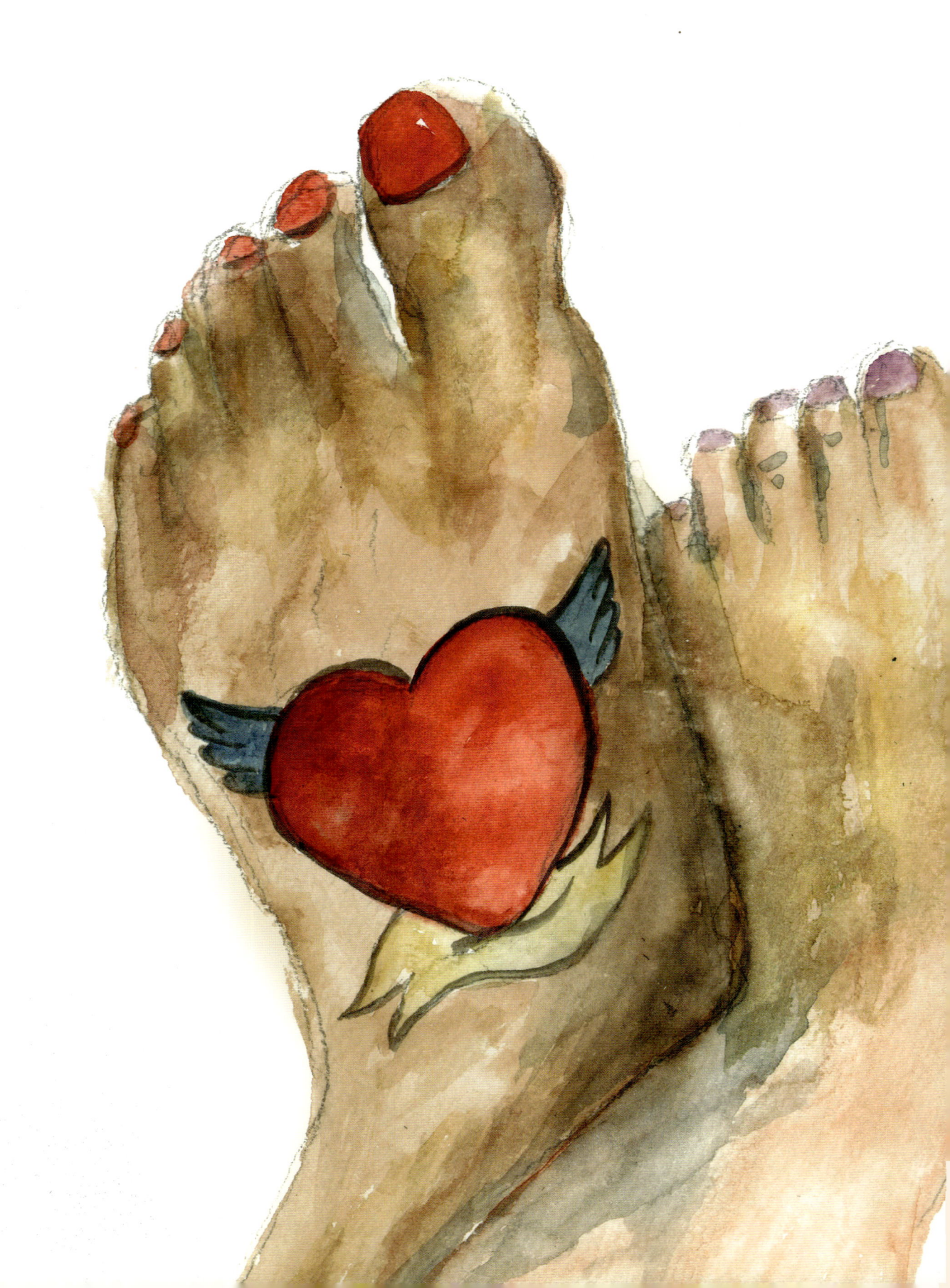

Every day my Mummy says, "I love my tattoos too but not as much as I love you."

Story and illustrations © 2014 Andy White @ CELEBRITIES ANONYMOUS.

All rights reserved. No part of this publication may be reproduced, stored in a retrieval system or transmitted in any form or by any means, electronic, mechanical, photocopying, recording or otherwise, without the prior written permission of the copyright holder.